Ours has always been a mutually rewarding friendship. We complement, support, like and generally listen to each other. The gratifying thing about reading his work now is that it grows with you. The older I get the more his poems reveal. I'm knocked out by the richness, the resonance, the generosity, the hard intelligence, the clarity, the passion and above all else, the great, great aching tenderness, which remains very much a part of who he is and what he means to me.

— Leonard Cohen

THE
LOVE
POEMS

THE
LOVE
POEMS

with reverence and delight

Irving Layton

mosaic press

I sang of thighs
I sang of breasts
I sang of shoulders
soft and black as soot
white and soft as cloud
and of curved lips
from which kisses
fell like rose petals
or flew like birds
wilder and wilder
I sang
as I grew older
and my loins wrinkled
like the forehead of a sage

Irving Layton

National Library of Canada Cataloguing in Publication Data

Layton, Irving, 1912-
    The love poems of Irving Layton

ISBN 0-88962-246-9

    1. Love poetry, Canadian (English) I. Title.

PS8523.A98L67 1984   C811′54   C80-009404-3
PR9199.3.L35L59 1984

Published by Mosaic Press, offices and warehouse at 1252 Speers Road, Units 1 and 2, Oakville, Ontario, L6L 5N9, Canada and Mosaic Press, PMB 145, 4500 Witmer Industrial Estates, Niagara Falls, NY, 14305-1386, U.S.A.

Mosaic Press acknowledges the assistance of the Canada Council and the Department of Canadian Heritage, Government of Canada for their support of our publishing programme.

Copyright © 2002 Irving Layton
First Published in 1984
Second printing 2002
Printed and Bound in Canada.
ISBN 0-88962-246-9

Le Conseil des Arts | The Canada Council
du Canada | for the Arts

Mosaic Press, in Canada:
1252 Speers Road, Units 1 & 2,
Oakville, Ontario
L6L 5N9
Phone/Fax: 905-825-2130
mosaicpress@on.aibn.com

Mosaic Press, in U.S.A.:
4500 Witmer Industrial Estates
PMB 145, Niagara Falls, NY
14305-1386
Phone/Fax: 1-800-387-8992
mosaicpress@on.aibn.com

CONTENTS

William Wordsworth was turned on by daffodils; I'm turned on by women. He saw their golden cups tossing beside the lake and stored the sight away in his mind to give him a lift whenever he felt vacant or depressed. I treasure the sight of firm-titted women walking on Avenue Road or St. Catharine St. He didn't pluck every daffodil he celebrated, nor have I every woman I've written poems for and now lay gratefully between the covers of this book.

My first poem was to a Grade Six teacher, Miss Benjamin. I yearned for her as only a horny pre-adolescent can who doesn't know what to do with his impulses, a riot of romanticism, idealism and burgeoning sensuality. I can still recall the excitement 'in the blood' I felt each time she entered the classroom, the dizziness and rapture I experienced when I looked up and saw her dimples, the lovely flush of her cheeks, her wavy brown hair. I used to pretend I had some difficulty with the arithmetic problem she had set the class to get her to bend over my desk so that I might see the crimson tinge that began at her chin and went right down to her tantalizing cleavage. Indeed, it has often occurred to me that every woman I've ever loved has been a materialization of Miss Benjamin, the fleshly incarnation of my boyhood desire for her.

Everything poets write about when they describe the delirium and ecstasy of love I have known from that time on. It has been difficult, sometimes impossible to give my attention to anything else; difficult for my mind with its penchant for abstractions and concepts to trick my heart into paying them the slightest heed or consideration. How can anyone who has known the intensities of love, its sudden spiraling upward to glory or downward to disaster and grief seriously entertain for any length of time notions on politics, religion, philosophy, literature, or even the meaner appetites and ambitions prevalent upon this planet. 'The food of love' is the only kind I've ever cared to eat, the only food I've ever hungered for. And talking about food: didn't I bolt down tiny black pellets of goatdung because I didn't want my first great love, watching me pick them up in her backyard, to think that her eleven-year-old gallant couldn't tell the difference between them and olives? Symbol or omen? Foretaste of things to come? Metaphor for the inescapable paradoxes of love? All these, of course.

I may have written two or three hundred love poems since my first one for Miss Benjamin. Many of them with more propriety could be called hate poems, for surely love and hate are two sides of the coin we call sexual interest or desire. For the present collection I've tried to call those poems that when put together in one volume will give the reader the startling thrill of a *déjà vu*. I want him to exclaim with understanding, amusement and sympathy: 'Yes, the writer of these verses knows what he's talking about. He has really been there, on those scarred slopes inhabited by *La Belle Dame Sans Merci*. He has paid for them in agony and exaltation for they have the authentic feel only personal knowledge can confer, without which poems are as lifeless as a pickled fetus. Only someone who has been on those slopes can have reproduced so faithfully the glory and carnage of the love emotion.'

What is the love emotion? When you are lost, and most yourself. Or to be comical and light-hearted about the matter: when you are a Sufi with Sophie on the sofa and you feel most alive, most intensely yourself and most generous.

When the antinomies of existence dissolve and dance into one another, merging into a music one hears at no other time; when clapping your hands with them as they melt into oneness you behold in a moment of ecstatic vision, the seamless unity of creation. At the moment dictator and tyrant are worms' food and you know with luminous certainty that all who hanker after titles and money are sick unhappy cripples the world would do beautifully without.

Let the philosophers rave on about the *summum bonum* and mystics about embracing God. They are still vertical humans and therefore even their adorations still have something aggressive about them. Humans in the horizontal position have always struck me as less likely to be violent and destructive. So I take my place beside the poets, and less arrogant than the philosopher or mystic, am prepared to find the greatest good and embrace God whenever I hold a woman in the act of love. It is then I know with assurance and inexpressible delight that whatever it is life promises us, this must be it; and that a universe containing this experience must have something grandly important going for it. That, finally, when all the subtractions are made, is what the love poems in this book are all about.

Irving Layton

For Miss Benjamin

LA MINERVE

And if I say my dog's vivid tongue
Clapped the frogs under their green fables
Or the rock's coolness under my hand
Told me clearly which way the sun passed

And if I say in a clean forest
I heard myself proclaimed a traitor
By the excellent cones for I thought
Where the good go, green as an apple

And if like our French grocer, Mailloux,
I lay these things on your white table
With a hot involuntary look,
And add a word about the first gods

I take satisfaction from your smile
And the inclination of your shoulder
Before the birds leave off their singing
And slow the dark fills up my eyes

But when you stand at night before me
Like the genius of this place, naked,
All my ribs most unpaganlike ache
With foolstruck Adam in his first wonder.

I would for your sake be gentle
Be, believe me, other than I am:
What, what madness is it that hurls me
Sundays against your Sunday calm?

True, there's enough gall in my ducts
To cover an area, and more:
But why you — free from evil, poor bird?
Why you — my heart and saviour?

I swear I'm damned to so hate and rage.
But your fair innocence is my guilt;
And the stream that you make clear
I must, to fog my image, fill with silt.

Bear with me, bear with me —
Your goodness, gift so little understood
Even by the angels I suppose
And by us here somewhat undervalued

Is what I hold to when madness comes.
It is the soft night against which I flare
Rocketwise, and when I fall
See my way back by my own embers.

Your figure, love,
curves itself
into a man's memory;
or to put it the way
a junior prof
at Mount Allison might,
Helen with her thick
absconding limbs
about the waist
of Paris
did no better.

Hell, my back's sunburnt
from so much love-making
in the open air.
The Primate (somebody
made a monkey of him)
and the Sanhedrin
(long on the beard, short
on the brain)
send envoys to say
they don't approve.
You never see them, love.
You toss me in the air
with such abandon,
they take to their heels and run.
I tell you
each kiss of yours
is like a blow on the head!

What luck, what luck to be loved
by the one girl
in this Presbyterian
country
who knows how to give
a man pleasure.

LETTER FROM A STRAW MAN

I loved you, Bobbo, even when you knuckled me
And pulled the straw out of my breast,
Pretending to weep yet secretly glad to note
How yellow and summer-dry the stuff was.

You will surely recall how amazed
We both were the straw was endless;
At the time I did not know it was your fingers
Made the straw grow there and blaze

Yellow in the fierce sunlight....How when
I once caught your cold blue eye
It first burned like sulphur, but affected
Let down a tear like a drop of dirty sea-water

Into my prized open chest; though after
That encounter of our eyes, your own —
The pitiful one — grew into a porcelain saucer
White and blind. That I could understand.

But why did you give great handfuls
To the visiting firemen? And when the mayor
Asked for some to decorate his fireplace,
Why did you not refuse? No, rather,

Plunging you green delicate fingers
Into my gaping breast you drew
Out for him the longest stalk
Which he snatched with a cough and a compelling eye.

I have left you for another,
Who wears black panties and is as crazy as the birds;
But when the straw comes away in her hands
She is careful to burn it immediately afterwords.

4   IRVING LAYTON

MISUNDERSTANDING

I placed
my hand
upon
her thigh.

By the way
she moved
away
I could see
her devotion
to literature
was not
perfect.

LATRIA

Give me, Dark One, these:
A woman's white knees
A woman's fine eyes
Her hot, lathered thighs

The nuptial embrace
The first look of love
A bird, sparrow or dove,
The unscheming face

Any bloom, a rose,
Creation's frenzy
The thrill of pity
— The rest is prose

LOVE'S DIFFIDENCE

Love is so diffident a thing.
I scoop up my hands with air;
I do not find it there
Nor in my friend's pleasure
Nor when the birds sing.

I am confused, forsaken.
I have lost the way.
Love's not as some men say
In woman's eyes, blue or grey;
Nor in kisses given and taken.

Love, I call out, find me
Spinning round in error.
Display your dank, coarse hair,
Your bubs and bulbous shoulder.
Then strike, witless bitch, blind me.

HOW POEMS GET WRITTEN

Like
a memory
torn
at the shoulder,
my darling
wears
the chemise
I gave her —
a wedding gift.

At night
I tap out
my poems
on her hip bone.

When
she can't
sleep
either
we write
the poem
together.

SACRAMENT BY THE WATER

How shall I sing the accomplished waters
Whose teeming cells make green my hopes
How shall the Sun at daybreak marry us
Twirling these waters like a hoop.

Gift of the waters that sing
Their eternal passion for the sky,
Your perfect beauty in a wave of tumult
Drops an Eden about your thighs.

Green is the singing singing water
And green is every joyous leaf
White myrtle's in your hand and in the other
The hair apple bringing life.

NIGHTFALL

We have taken the night
like a Persian black cat
into bed with us;
your fingers stoking body's heat
are the glittering red
glassware of my childhood,
are scents suddenly
remembered and pungent;
dark rivers flow under your hair
as under remote bridges.
I feel with my hands
the cool rain bark of you limbs.

Afterwards lying on our backs
like pillowed sovereigns
we decree space
and allow thought and the room's objects
to separate us;
abstract and personal
we turn
in the round cavity of sleep

BERRY PICKING

Silently my wife walks on the still wet furze
Now darkgreen the leaves are full of metaphors
Now lit up is each tiny lamp of blueberry.
The white nails of rain have dropped and the sun is free.

And whether she bends or straightens to each bush
To find the children's laughter among the leaves
Her quiet hands seem to make the quiet summer hush —
Berries or children, patient she is with these.

I only vex and perplex her; madness, rage
Are endearing perhaps put down upon the page;
Even silence daylong and sullen can then
Enamour as restraint or classic discipline.

So I envy the berries she puts in her mouth,
The red and succulent juice that stains her lips;
I shall never taste that good to her, nor will they
Displease her with a thousand barbarous jests.

How they lie easily for her hand to take,
Part of the unoffending world that is hers;
Here beyond complexity she stands and stares
And leans her marvellous head as if for answers.

No more the easy soul my childish craft deceives
Nor the simpler one for whom yes is always yes;
No, now her voice comes to me from a far way off
Though her lips are redder than the raspberries.

BARGAIN

In fourteen years
        of married bliss
not once have I been disloyal
to my wife;
and you, I am told, are still
a virgin.

If you are set
        to barter your maidenhead
for my unheard-of fidelity,
call me between three and five tomorrow
and it is done.

RAIN

The wind blew hard in the trees
And palegreen was the wet grass;
I love you, Love, my Sweet said
And gave her false mouth to kiss.

Huge leopard spots the rain put
On the stone near where we sat;
An obscure song at our feet
Sang the troubled rivulet.

In front the black road went by,
A panther in search of prey;
Between some mouldering firs
I lay down her bleeding corse.

The wind blew hard in the trees
And screeched in the low briars;
I loved you truly, I said
And kissed her false dead mouth.

The rain fell, decaying eyes
And small ears; how green the moss!
Let her red lips kiss the rot
In their last quiver of death.

The white rain shall knit her shroud
And clean my hands of her blood;
The cottage on the round lake
Blind that eye like a cataract.

BECAUSE MY CALLING IS SUCH

Because by calling is such
I lose myself whole days
In some foul cistern or ditch,
How should mere woman's love reach
Across the lampless silence
For the sake of that craze
Made blind Homer dance —

I, crouched in the rainless air
And choking with the dust?
Yet so bowed, the readier
To kiss your palm, my finger
Touching your fabulous face
Beyond all error and lust
In all that dark place.

For the trove of images
One gathers in the dark,
The dark that's piled with refuse
I shall not curse the bright phrase,
Coronal of my eclipse;
Though had you wed a clerk
He'd have your red lips.

Not driven like a lazar
From his house and children,
His embraces as he were
Frog on your white sheets, my dear,
Made mock of and rejected:
Who'd turn had you chosen
A prince on your bed.

HOLIDAY

"Quebec roads are damned tricky," he shouted
To his wife out on the lake rowing;
"Adrien's girl will travel a-ways with me,
But I do not know why or where she's going."

He saw his stolid wife drop from the boat
And stand, the water around her flowing;
And he saw the bent father near the shore
Where the farm tumbled into weed, mowing.

The sensual sun was mounted on a hill.
His passion too was mounting, O growing
With each quick step in unison they took;
And where the road dipped, he felt like crowing.

Black horsedung, stones, and yellow butterflies;
A young bull and his herd of cows lowing;
The white cock fastened on top the roadside cross
That could not tell which way the wind was blowing.

DIVORCE

What is it about divorce
brings an estranged couple closer?
Here we are, Boschka, nearly twenty years later
reading our poems and stories to each other;
the fire blazes: its warmth is not greater
than what's in our souls;
we listen, comment, approve
and laugh like two grey-haired children.
Why now, not then, the love we display
exchanging news of friends and the universe
after a morning of rain and mist?
Arm-around-waist we walk, talk,
and always with the ease of those
who know their words and actions please.

Someone up there must be an ironist!
Or is it, seeing our soaped heads
in the mirror
who in hell wants to add more discord
to the general futility?
Let the dropped crabapple moulder where it falls,
the seed will clutch and break the soil.
Is that what love is: to care knowing
stars and blossoms flare to extinction?
We've separated wide the fingers of our hands
and let fall through them egotism, illusion, pride:
dear, dear Boschka, how tenderly now
our fingers entwine and hold.

FOR PRISCILLA

Sitting by this idiot
radio
on a windy night
I recall you
tight and impervious
as a pebble
and prototype
of your unmagnanimous sex,
a female hyena
of the spirit
who sniffed the delicious foetor
from my rotting psyche;
and I think whether
the neat dot
of you posterior
incrassating
like a gourd
into the steamy vegetation
of your middle years
will traitorously swallow up
the wedge-shaped virgule
of your back, once,
ah, firm as a ballet-dancer's.

SONG FOR A LATE HOUR

No one told me
to beware your bracelets,
the winds I could expect
from your small breasts.
No one told me
the tumult of your hair.
When a lock touched me
I knew the sensations
of shattering glass.

Your kissings put
blue water around me.
I would look at you
with bold Cretan mirth:
I would forget
I am a cringing semite,
a spaniel suffering
about your tight skirts.

I slabber for your rippling
hips, your white shoulders.
I am sick
with love of you. Girl, o girl,
let our washed limbs make
a perverse Star of David
and cones of flesh,
Cythera all night
at my silvered back.

WOMAN

Vain and not to trust
unstable as wind,
as the wind ignorant;
shallow, her laugh
jarring my mended teeth.
I spit out
the loose silver
from my aching mouth.

With candid gaze
she meets my jealous
look, and is false.
Yet I am lost, lost.
Beauty and pleasure,
fatal gifts,
she brings in her thighs,
in her small amorous body.

O not remembering
her derision of me,
I plunge like a corkscrew
into her softness,
her small wicked body
and there, beyond reproach,
I roar like a sick lion
Between her breasts.

MODERN LOVE

Saying your enterprise cannot fail:
You have no drab inhibitions
And your lovers no intelligence

Saying you are fantastical bawdy shameless
Exquisite false amorous
Your lips breasts and thighs in perfect control

Saying you know how to delight each of us
For I you swear am your true love
And the other you have promised marriage

I impaled you on your rumpled bed

NAUSICAA

'I'm the sort of girl
        you must first tell you love.'
'I love you,' I said.
She gave herself to me then
    and I enjoyed her on her perfumed bed.

By the gods, the pleasure in her small
        wriggling body was so great,
    I had spoken no lecherous falsehood.
Now not nor my beloved,
        such is our heat,
can wait for either words or scented sheet
but on her or my raincoat go roughly to it.

UNDINE

Your body to hold, your perfect breasts.
Your lips; your hips under my pregnant hands
    That when they move, why, they're snakes
Sliding, and hiding near your golden buttocks.

Then as your great engines of love begin
Intestinal, furious, submarine
    They spark into small bites
Whose hot spittle inundates all my deserts.

And I'm like water in a scoop of stone
Kissed into absence by a drying sun;
    Or I'm dried Sahara sand
Wanting your wetness over me without end.

So possessed, so broken's my entire self
No rosy whipcord, love, can bind my halves
    When queen you squat; you moisten
My parched nipples into a blazing garden.

And I your paramour-Paracelsus
Fish a soul for you from between my loins;
    You shudder in my embrace
And all your wetness takes the form of tears.

BY ECSTASIES PERPLEXED

By that, by this, by sharp ecstasies perplexed,
illumined, a saint streaked with foibles,
    I wore at the heart a hairshirt of fire,
wrapped my thighs in a loincloth of bees.

Honour foreswore and talent, and with these
burnished those bluedyed baubles which hang
    amorously from sad and arid bantam trees
in one-room apartments cheaply furnished.

Yet now with lust and indignation spent
and even remorse and other troubles
    I ask whether by deliberate will I went
or frenzy at a woman's beauty.

And cannot answer. But recall
a flaxen-haired boy five years old
    who one bad night put fire to his gown
and watched the flames about him rise blue and gold.

THE DAY AVIVA CAME TO PARIS

The day you came naked to Paris
The tourists returned home without their guidebooks,
The hunger in their cameras finally appeased.

Alone once more with their gargoyles, the Frenchmen
Marvelled at the imagination that had produced them
And once again invited terror into their apéritifs.
Death was no longer exiled to the cemeteries.

In their royal gardens where the fish die of old age,
They perused something else besides newspapers
— A volume perhaps by one of their famous writers.
They opened their hearts to let your tender smile defrost them;
Their livers filled with an unassuageable love of justice.
They became the atmosphere around them.

They learned take money from Americans
Without a feeling of revulsion towards them;
And to think of themselves
As not excessively subtle or witty.
"*Au diable* with Voltaire," they muttered,
"Who was a national calamity.
Au diable with *la République*.
(A race of incurable petits bourgeois, the French
are happiest under a horse under a man)
Au diable with *la Monarchie!*
We saw no goddesses during either folly;
Our bald-headed savants never had told us
Such a blaze of public hair anywhere existed."
And they ordered the grandson of Grandma Moses
To paint it large on the dome of le Sacré-Coeur.

My little one, as if under those painted skies
It was again 1848,
They leaped as one mad colossal Frenchman from their
     café Pernods
Shouting, "*Vive l'Australienne!*
Vive Layton who brought her among us!
Let us erect monuments of black porphyry to them!
Let us bury them in the Panthéon!)"

(*Pas si vite, messieurs*; we are still alive)

And when, an undraped Jewish Venus,
You pointed to a child, a whole slum starving in her eyes,
Within earshot of the Tuileries,
The French who are crazy or catholic enough
To place, facing each other, two tableaux
— One for the Men of the Convention, and one puffing
     the Orators of the Restoration —
At once made a circle wide as the sky around you
While the Mayor of the 5th Arondissement
Addressed the milling millions of Frenchmen:

"See how shapely small her adorable ass is;
Of what an incredible pink rotundity each cheek.
A bas Merovingian and *Valois!*
A bas Charlemagne and *Henri Quatre!*
For all the adulations we have paid them
In our fabulous histoires
They cannot raise an erection between them. Ah,
For too long has the madness of love
Been explained to us by sensualists and curés.
A bas Stendhal! A bas Bossuet!

"Forever and forever, from this blazing hour
All Paris radiates from Aviva's nest of hair
— Delicate hatchery of profound delights —
From her ever-to-be-adored *Arche de Triomphe!*
All the languors of history
Take on meaning clear as a wineglass or the belch of an angel
Only if thought of as rushing
On the wings of a rhinoceros towards this absorbing event.
Voyeurs, voyez! The moisture of her delicate instep
Is a pool of love
Into which sheathed in candy paper
Anaesthetized politicians drop from the skies!"
(Word Jugglery of course, my Sweet; but the French love it
— Mistake it in fact for poetry)

And the applaudissements and bravos
Bombinating along the Boulevard Saint-Germain
Made the poor docile Seine
Think our great Atlantic was upon it.
It overflowed with fright into the bookstalls
And sidewalk cafés.
Fifteen remaining Allemands with their cameras
Were flushed down the Rue Pigalle.

And when you were raised up
Into my hairy arms by the raving emotional crowds
Waving frenzied bottles of Beaujolais
And throwing the corks away ecstatically
(Not saving them!)
It was, my Love, my Darling,
As if someone had again ordered an advance
Upon the Bastille
Which we recalled joyously, face to face at last,
Had yielded after only a small token resistance.

THE DARK NEST

Once and once only
With clear eyes I saw
Mine your false heart was,
Mine your insolent brow.

Your tongue lolled between
My teeth, a red root;
Caressing mine it
Folded up my queer breath.

Your bright member twined
Once about my mind,
Became in that dark nest
A dark bisected post.

Whose pliant furlongs
Far reached down to where
Impurity's duff
For strength, guilts engender.

Raving you plucked it
From my face, revealed
Shiny on its nib
Hell's puerperal bead.

I KNOW THE DARK AND HOVERING MOTH

For vilest emissary of death
I know the dark and hovering moth
Whose furred wings overwhelm the sun;
And the blind minnows that cannot swim.

Oh, a fat black moth was my first wife.
She sat her weight on my greenest leaf.
Another moth was so fair a prize,
Melted my manhood into her eyes.

William Blake spied the vanishing heel,
Made all the white stars in heaven reel.
I heard his wild, dismayed shout.
Rib by rib Urizen lugged me out.

Now at early dawn, my heart with joy,
Like any carefree holiday boy
I look at the minnows in the pond
And catch and kill them: they make no sound.

Lovely Aviva, shall we crush moths?
Geldings stone till we're out of breath?
Wipe the minnows from the goat-god's brow?
He hears their screams; he rejoices now.

For sun throbs with sexual energy;
The meadows bathe in it, each tall tree.
The sweet dark graves give up their dead.
Love buries the stale fish in their stead.

From crows we'll brew a cunning leaven;
From harsh nettles: lock them in a poem.
The virtuous reading it at once
Will change into rimed and sapless stumps.

My proud Love we'll water them, embrace
Over their unleaving wretchedness:
Till snakes cavort in gardens and sing
Melic praises for each mortal thing;

And from Lethean pond beneath a scarp
There rush the vigorous hunting carp
At whose gorping jaws and obscene mouth
Flit the vulnerable black-winged moths;

Poets, each the resurrected Christ,
Move like red butterflies through the mist
To where the shafts, the sloping shafts of Hell,
The globed sun enclose like a genital.

DIVINITY

Were I a clumsy poet
I'd compare you to Helen;
Ransack the mythologies
Greek, Chinese, and Persian

For a goddess vehement
And slim; one with form as fair.
Yet find none. O, love, you are
Lithe as a Jew peddler

And full of grace. Such lightness
Is in your step, instruments
I keep for the beholder
To prove you walk, not dance.

Merely to touch you is fire
In my head; my hair becomes
A burning bush. When you speak,
Like Moses I am dumb

With marvelling, or like him
I stutter with pride and fear:
I hold, Love, divinity
In my changed face and hair.

FOR AVIVA, BECAUSE I LOVE HER

I saw a spider eating a huge bee.

First he ate my limbs;
and then he removed my head, feasting
    on the quivering jellies of my eyes
and on what passes among bees for ears.

And though dead,
I could feel, with each morsel he had,
that he enjoyed his repast
    and I was glad.

Afterwards he sliced me down the middle,
exposing my insides
    to the burning mid-day heat;
and slowly the voluptuous spider
feasted on my jewelled organs,
abolishing them one by one,
till I was all gone, all swallowed up,
    except for my love of you:

My radiant wings — these, ah, these
he did not touch
but left glinting in the sun.

ANDROGNE

Were Death a woman I should never die.
So jealous is my loving wife that I
Could look upon a passing hearse and sneer
At this dumb show of frail mortality.
For what from Death would I have then to fear

Who might not even by her darkest guile,
Her frowned commands, her most sensual smile,
Tear me from Love? Tell me, who'd encroach
On her whose fingers stiffen to a file,
Seeing a woman from afar approach?

No, certainly I shall live forever;
For my dear wife will be immortal too
As one whom Death, androgynous lover,
Rages against my jealousy to woo.
Only by dread compact shall we be free
For waiting Death to ravish her and me.

ETERNAL RECURRENCE

Even that leaf as it falls
Will one day fall again
Be sad, be gaily crimson
And flutter while a bird calls

And the bough on which he sits
Lengthen into the dark
While my staring eyes mark
How between the trees your shadow flits

And in my mind image of your face
Vain and angry as you said
Your words and turned away your head:
They will come again, the pain and grace

A million years hence; and from that bough
The same bird calling,
The same crimson leaf falling
And I writing and crying — then as now

THE AIR IS SULTRY

The air is sultry.
    So is my soul.

The coffee is bitter.
    So are my thoughts.

The cigarette is stale.
    Ditto my emotions.

There's a filthy hole in the wall.
    There's one in my heart.

It is going to rain.
    The rain can't help me.

My darling has run off with another man.
    Who cares?

I hear her knock on the door.
    She brings me suffering.

She tells me she loves me.
    I tell her I adore her.

The air is sultry.
    So is my soul.

IF I LIE STILL

If I lie still
the light from the leaves
will drop on my hands and knees

Fire will envelop me
yet I won't burn

I shall hear the silence plainly
while the stream flows into my veins
and out again

Small wild animals will no longer fear me,
but bring their young
to tickle my heels,
nuzzle in my armpits

I shall know love without disquiet
— without passion

For a thousand years
I shall lie like this
with my head toward the sun

Till knowledge and power
have become one;
then I shall write a single verse,
achieve one flawless deed

Then lie down again
to become like this shallow
stone under my hand,
and let my face
be covered with grass

To be pulled out by the roots
by what raging hermit,
his breast torn apart as mine now?

MAHOGANY RED

Once, a single hair could bind me to you;
had you told me: 'Jump
from the tallest building'
I'd have raced up on three elevators
and come down on my skull;
from the land of wailing ghosts
I'd have mailed you a fragment of skullbone
initialled by other desperate men
had despaired of ever pleasuring their lovers.
Once, pleasure expanded in my phallus
like a thin, excruciating column of mercury;
when it exploded in my brain
it was like a movie I once saw
where the earth is grabbed by the sun
and fried black;
or another ice age arrived on snow
and I danced hot and bare and alone
on a lost glacier,
hairy mammoths circling around me.
Once, I was a galley-slave
lying stripped in all your fragrant ports;
a tickle in my groin
made your skin a torment to me,
and I dived into the dimples of your knees
when you stretched naked and sexy on your bed.
Godhead, the Marxist revolution, History
that is so full of tombs and tears,
I stuffed them all up your golden rectum
and sewed up their sole escape route
with frantic kisses sharper than needles.
Now, without any warning
you are a middle-aged woman
who has tinted her hair mahogany red;
one of your front teeth, I notice, is discoloured grey;

I notice, too, how often you say
'phony' and 'artificial'
and wonder each time if you're not projecting.
Yes, suddenly you are a woman
no different from other women;
a little less nasty perhaps,
a little less insincere,
less contemptuous of the male sex,
wistful and dissatisfied in your contempt,
still hankering for greatness, the dominant man,
his flowing locks all the spread-out sky you want;
unfair, conscienceless, your bag of woman's tricks close by,
hard beset, as women in all ages have been,
needing to make your way, to survive,
to be praised immoderately,
to be nibbled by a lover's amorous teeth,
to procreate...
vain of your seductive wiggle when you walk away from me,
of your perfect breasts displaying nipples
I wanted to devour
and die choking, their pink tips tickling my throat;
vain of the fiery pennant under your chin
pinned there by your latest lover.

The bulb in my brain
once ignited and kept aglow
by genital electricity
lies smashed to bits.
I look out at the world with cool, aware eyes;
I pick out the pieces of grey glass from my brain;
I hold them all in my trembling hand.

Only a god could put them together again
and make them light up with sexual ecstasy,
but he lies sewn up in your golden rectum
huddled beside History and the Marxist revolution.
It is sad to be an atheist,
sadder yet to be one with a limp phallus.
Who knows
maybe if I had swung and knocked out
your one discoloured tooth
I would still love you, your little girl's grin,
small gap in your jaw
(who knows, who knows)
and not have wanted to write
this bitter, inaccurate poem.

HILLS AND HILLS

The hills
remind me
of you

Not because
they curve soft and warm
lovely and firm
under the Greek sun

Or flow
towards the horizon
in slow limpid waves
falling away mysteriously
at the edge of the sea

So that I can only surmise
their being there
beyond my gaze
and stare into the greyness

But because
a long time ago
you stared at them
as I am staring now

LETTER TO A LOST LOVE

We can speak the words, my dear, of forgiveness
but only our actions could have healed us;
now we're both doomed to incompleteness
and to grimace as though with Bell's palsy.
I was just beginning to see through words,
with false bottoms and sawed-up ladies,
the will-o-wisps he'd have me take for real;
you, at last, to see me with love's insight,
the compassion that only wisdom gives.
Now we're like the absurd figures of Pompei
forever arrested in a vague stance,
a gesture never to be completed,
dumb in the stillness our lava's made.
How words have fooled me all these years,
deceived me like the witches on the heath:
yet poor Macbeth was a poet also
and only poets can misconstrue where
the Banquos without a stitch of imagination
see only hideous misshapen hags about
and rightly smell the mess they're cooking.
If a Banquo croaks it's only because
an assassin's prosaic poignard
gets him in the gut; it's never dreams,
or ambition, the mad reaching out for greatness
and distinction, an immortal name
defying old Skull-and-Bones bringing
oblivion in his grinding white molars.

So farewell, my love, a long, long farewell;
maybe the Atlantic will wipe out the guilt,
the knowledge of wrongs done and suffered;
maybe in some other life I'll be asked
to cover the fourth wall of Paridise
and unlike del Sarto not have to choose
betwixt love and art but, blessed, have both.
But in the here and now I have a misery
to last my life and if I don't tear a hole
in my heart as wide and deep as its pain
it's because I've Byron's way of seeing things
and think death even more absurd than life
and once dead there's no more laughing then.

AVIVA

Dear wife, it is not your beauty
though beautiful you be
nor is it your warm grace and intelligence
that sweep me to your feet
to be kept a captive there
by your smiles, your brightening glance

Granted, you are lovely beyond compare:
still, unprincipled poet that I am
it is for your name alone I adore
and follow you around on prayerful knees
though, entrancing one, you should leave me
at the wide mouth of Hades

Fiery Catullus had his Lesbia
and the gentle Tibullus, his Delia
Propertius mooned for Cynthia
while the great Ovid, sensual and wise,
swooned in faultless verse
for his incomparable Corinna

I, swiftly scaling
my heraldic ladder in an ethnic slum
I, Irving Layton, with these Latin elegists
shall be numbered in times to come
having doxologized you, lovely Aviva,
whose vernal name is loveliest of all

FOR MUSIA'S GRANDCHILDREN

I write this poem
for your grandchildren
for they will know of your loveliness
only from hearsay,
from yellowing photographs
spread out on table and sofa
for a laugh.

When arrogant
with the lovely grace you gave their flesh
they regard your dear frail body pityingly,
your time-dishonoured cheeks
pallid and sunken
and those hands
that I have kissed a thousand times
mottled by age
and stroking a grey ringlet into place,
I want them suddenly
to see you as I saw you
— beautiful as the first bird at dawn.

Dearest love, tell them
that I, a crazed poet all his days
who made woman
his ceaseless study and delight,
begged but one boon
in this world of mournful beasts
that are almost human:
to live praising your marvellous eyes
mischief could make glisten
like winter pools at night
or appetite put a fine finish on.

CREATION

I fashioned you:
Composed you between darkness and dawn.

You are my best-made poem,
The one I laboured longest over.

What does one do with a poem?
One gives it to the world.

Go, darling, delight others
As you have delighted me.

Bring your fragrant freshness
To lover and lover.

In their loins sow madness and fever
That my fame may endure forever.

WITH THE MONEY I SPEND

With the money I spend on you
I could buy ice cream for Korean kings.
I could adopt a beggar
    and clothe him in scarlet and gold.
I could leave a legacy of dolls and roses
        to my grandchildren.
Why must you order expensive Turkish cigarettes?
And why do you drink only the most costly champagne?
The Leninists are marching on us.
Their eyes are inflamed with social justice.
Their mouths are contorted with the brotherhood of man.
Their fists are heavy with universal love.
They have not read a line of Mayakovsky's poems
    for twelve whole months.
The deprivation has made them desperate.
With staring eyeballs they hold off
    waiting for the ash from your cigarette to fall.
That is the signal.
When the ash crumbles, the man with the smallest forehead
    will smash a cracked hourglass, the sound
        amplified into a thousand manifestos.
Can you not see them? Can you not hear them?
Already they are closing in on us.
Your fragrant body means nothing to them.
Under your very eyes, velvet and remarkable,
    they intone that Beauty is not absolute.
They shout for an unobstructed view of your shoulders,
    your proud and beautiful head gone.
They will break your arms and slender legs
    into firewood.

The golden delicate hairs I have kissed
    into fire a thousand times
        will blaze more brightly;
But who will bend down to gather the flames
    into their mouth?
Who will follow their white light into eternity?
Because I love you better
    than artichokes and candles in the dark,
I shall speak to them.
Perhaps they will overlook your grace for my sake,
    ignore the offending perfection of your lips.
Perhaps, after all, you and I will start
    a mass conversion into elegance.
I will tell them my father made cheese
    and was humble and poor all his life,
And that his father before him turned ill
    at the mere sight of money;
And that a certain remote ancestor of mine
    never saw money at all,
        having been born blind.
On my mother's side, they were all failures.
Calliopes will sound for my undistinguished lineage
And the aroused Leninists will at once guess
    I am a fool in love, a simpleton,
        an ensnared and deranged proletarian
With no prospects but the wind which exposes
    my terrible hungers to them,
My counter-revolutionary appetite to be lost
    from all useful labour
        in your arms hair thighs navel;
And parting the clouds, one solitary star
    to show them where I am slain
Counting the gold coins
    for your Turkish cigarettes and costly champagne.

A STRANGE TURN

A moment ago, in my embrace
She rode me like a Joan of Arc;
Then seeing my fifty-year-old face
Where Time's acids had burned deep their mark,
My head of hair coloured gray and rust,
And my old eyes wise with genial lust
She stiffened and held herself in check.

I felt her limbs slacken at my side
As sweetly she kissed my wrinkled neck;
Desire unspent had all but fled
Leaving behind its wraith, mere sentiment,
That poised her astride me motionless.
Ah, if my flesh were but firm, not loose,
And I were young, how she'd ride and ride!

YOU AND THE 20TH CENTURY

On the one hand, dear girl, there's
this brutal stinking 20th century;
on the other hand there is you
or rather your incredible sapphire eyes

Let me do some rapid mental arithmetic:
the big wars one and two, some smaller ones,
Auschwitz and Vorkuta, of course Hiroshima,
revolutions, massacres, executions and — Stalin

And as companion piece though lacking
the Georgian's consummate hypocrisy, Hitler;
such two you may be sure will never again be seen:
and even History can repeat her masterstrokes

Though once again the merciless pinheads are loose
in the streets, man-loving idealists are sniffing
human blood; the weak resenting their weakness
dividing neatly into demagogues and murderers

It's a familiar enough story, God knows
who uses the same old ploys to push us on
to meet the Messiah, i.e. death of course
who alone brings peace, redemption from lies and murder

I endure both what I know as memory
and as learning as well as the day's outrages
hustling us inescapably into vulgarity and serfdom
because not otherwise can I know your beauty

Yet, love, when I see your incredibly lovely eyes
wise as an old woman's, bright with mischief,
it seems I can pick up the day as calmly as a child
picks up a forgotten toy from his littered floor

FANATIC IN SAN FELIU

They said it wouldn't rain
after the 21st of June
in San Feliu.
It did. It rained every day.
And oftener.
They said I would find
and finger
multitudes of young girls
with tight butts
and tits like pistols
cocked to go off in your face:
lies, the fantasies
of incarcerated lechers.
They said there would be festivals
every day, beginning
with the day of my coming:
to date, a Spanish sparkplug
exploded in the empty street
— nothing else.

Someone — was it you?—
hijacked
the crowds, the fierce and arrogant
Catalan dancers,
the cruel women with dazzling mouths
and whisked them off
to a neighbouring town
where everyone is making love
to lascivious girls of fifteen
— banners and streamers
are everywhere
and people all night
are drinking and singing
in the festooned squares.

Now under this soaked awning
beside an abandoned aquarium
full of crawling baby lobsters
whose rubbery black eyes
I imagine moles
on your lifeless breasts
are only some empty chairs
and myself,
a lonely fanatic with images
of your white faraway body
and corrupt mouth
to torment him this rainswept
cold evening
while the high and swelling wind
howls with his terrible sickness.

BLUE AND LOVELY, MY LOVE

Blue and lovely, my Love,
are the butterflies on your shoulders.
I heard you sing for them
when you were false to everything
including the snapshot of my grandmother
I gave you under the evening star.
They shoveled me into the cold earth
but I heard your singing;
I was ash but I still heard you.
It is no longer you or your voice
that torments me;
It's the blue butterflies looking for me
between the tall grasses
that grow from stilled desire and disdain
as if they were my hands reaching for your face.

THE WORM

The filthy rain
blackens the street

Knowing that you lie
this afternoon
whimpering in another man's
arms

I picture you stretched out,
a stiffened corpse

And your cold vagina
extruding
a solitary pink
worm.

THE SEDUCTION

First he knocks her down
   by assaulting her soul;
telling her she's vain, superficial,
and adding — to drive his point home —
   that she's frivolous
and terribly, terribly selfish.

She takes the bait
   like the blonde fish she is
and for whole weeks goes about
beating her lovely breasts
   till her niplets
look like congealed drops of blood.
O she's full of remorse,
   full of remorse for all
her past egocentric, thoughtless ways,
and she sighs and cries a great deal.

Remorse in women
   is a sure-fire aphrodisiac:
they can't bear to be thought less than perfect
and so their contrition
is actually a variant form of vanity
and vanity is a great quickener
   of the sexual appetite.
Everything about them, in fact, is false
except passion; only in their desire
for intercourse are they completely sincere.

This with a priest's cunning my rival knew
   as well as I myself now do:
Judging her sufficiently broken,
   humbled and contrite,
he thinks the moment exactly right
   to toss her some small compliment
as one tosses a bone to a famished bitch.

(He praised, I think, her fidelity to friends).
The colour swoops back into her cheeks,
her eyes put on their fetching impertinence,
for the first time in weeks she laughs.

She's grateful,
    and when a woman is grateful
she has many ways of expressing her sense
of the occasion
but naturally prefers the easiest
    and most pleasant one.
In this, my Lucy was no exception.
Her gratitude is immense,
yet no greater than the provocation had been
which now stretches her out
    in perfect humility
while he rises beautifully to the occasion.
He dazes her with sweet, forgiving kisses
and all the long and lazy afternoon
    they're mutual as thieves in a cell
and, ah, tender as they come.

COAL

I no longer understand the simplest things

When I loved that woman
and my nights were sleepless
for thinking of her kisses
that fell on my body live coals,
for all my great art
I was inarticulate
and I could not praise her
but moaned like a swollen filthy stream
under her amorous fingers.

Now that I loathe her
and hourly wish her dead,
the remembering of her lips
fires my heart, my imagination
so that I see her kisses
drop from her curved mouth
black coal from a filthy coalsack.
My thoughts flow endlessly
and I cannot stop writing for her
poem after poem.

FOR LOUISE, AGE 17

She came to us recommended
By the golden minutes and by nothing else;
Her skin glowed, sang with the compliments
Which these same minutes paid her.

Her hair burned like a yellow fire
To celebrate the strange beauty of her face;
Herself, she walked unconscious
Of the need she started in us to praise, admire

The elegance we found in us
Like a vein of rare silver when we saw her;
But all our thoughts were caught in the compass
Of her royal arms and we sank down

Into the dark where the blood sings after dark,
Into the light because it was the light,
Into the clear valley where her body was made,
Her beauty had lain, now resurrected

Raised by the minutes, which start, slay,
Their ivory hafts fiery with sun-motes
Which, crying, we seized to make an immortal ring
For beauty which is its own excuse and never dies.

DANS LE JARDIN

Dearest girl, my hands are too fond of flesh
For me to speak to you; and you are too tall
For me to think you beautiful, though beautiful
You are. You are some other's fortunate wish

Though alone and your idle limbs inviting.
If I should call to you, give you this verse
And later caress your thighs with these fingers
You would rise like a wraith, like some wan Viking

Come from the North, mists upon her shoulders.
Your eyes are too grave and too luminous
And pledge but one cold nocturnal kiss,
Their gaze putting out the fires that it stirs

Till I hear bells, a slowly dying sound,
Where no bells are; how then should I suppose
You passionately flinging off skirt and blouse
And letting my squat body pin you to the ground?

So as you move your blanket and thin buttocks
To catch the failing sunlight on your face,
I watch you from my stationary place,
My limbs as immovable as these planted rocks

And think of Fate and of your immoderate height
And of your spoiling gauntness; and of what blind
Excuse to making the ceremonious stars who'll find
Our bodies uncoupled by the coming night.

FOR MY GREEN OLD AGE

Your eyes, lips, voice:
these I could withstand;
but when you unbuttoned your blouse
to show me the pink shapeliness
            of your breasts,
my fingers like five sentinels
trembled with surprise;
warts and all my wisdom I sang away
and the cigarette's irresolute ash
splashed on my stiff trouser leg like water.

Was it a beautiful woman's malice
or her mockery
made you turn and say,
standing there like Eve's naked daughter:
        "Since you cannot find the ashtray,
how will you know what's between my thighs?"

Whatever, and who cares:
when I am a greyhead full of years
I shall tell the priests and rabbis
about your gaiety
and of how to keep my hand from trembling
you pressed it between your thighs.

THE WAY TO GO

Envy, lust, my rare-scented queen,
  rule men's lives; lust declines
for time and use turn the love-muscle flabby
but envy takes a man right to the grave

Surviving I note wrily in the noblest
  it troubles me like wens
and deep pitmarks on the face of a woman
once loved for her beauty

I pray my last days on earth be mad
  with sexual desire
so that virgins scatter at my coming
like timorous pigeons and sparrows

And when I die, die my Love
  with a lascivious image
in my head: my hand slowly
ascending your hot uncovered thigh

TALK AT TWILIGHT

Night
slides down
the smooth, immense
tooth
of day
like firemen
down a pole
and everywhere
stamps out
the garish light.

My love's voice
crackling
under my ear
I smother it
in a blanket
of silence
soft
with tenderness
and irony.

FOR MISS CEZANNE

Last night I dreamt
        of one of your canvases;
the figures, obscure and innocent,
had stripped and slipped off
to be promptly arrested for indecent exposure
and smoking pot;
also for stealing packets of chewing gum
from drugstore counters that suspected nothing.
Your whole disorderly world,
        messy with life —
the bourgeois' nightmare, the civilized man's
despair —
jiggled crazily under my blessing
twin-branched arms, all ten fingers
lit up like chandelier crystals
        washed by whisky:
and waiting
                waiting
for the feel of your heavy flesh,
for the sadness, gayety, surrender, tenderness
and Being final as a root
which of all loves men have known
stretching in a luminous black line
to Eve's last, most radiant ringlet
you alone bring and give.

INSOMNIA

After the bath
you lay on the bed
exposing layers
of beautiful washed skin
we both stared at in surprise;
long strands of hair, shiny and damp
under the yellow lamplight,
fell over your shoulders:
they made two exclamation marks
with your stiffened nipples.

And gently you fell asleep
at my side;
while I, my sweet, stayed awake
all night
who had your uncovered beauty
to think about,
your nipples troubling me
in the night
like two mysterious asterisks.

WINTER LYRIC

Winter knows the good are poor,
that talent goes begging warmth
from ice and snow.
I hear my soul howling in the wind.
How can I write a poem to you
when you leave nothing for my pen?
There isn't a nib's thickness
between wish and fact, between
ideal and actuality.
If I give my imagination a head start,
you always catch up with me
— especially in bed!

It's almost 3 P.M.
The yahoos in the tavern
are more restless
than usual.
I'd better go home and tell you
how perfect you are.

My girl waits for me
with soup and wide-apart eyes;
she too has hankerings for immortality;
this morning I left her
inventing the figure
of a cosmonaut
on a crowded beach
— doubtless he was looking for her!

The seas is gentle this morning
(it has not yet read the newspaper)
and gives only the most restrained send-offs
to the stunted *borzoi*
scrambling towards the shore;
later it will roll
from the lidded shore
like a huge inflamed eyeball.

I pull words out of my fountain pen
and stare at the beach girls
in their bikinis,
scrupulously having
the passion they generate
in my loins;
when I return for my noonday meal
I'll offer it to my talented girl
and lay my poems
before her wide-apart eyes.

PRELUDE

Like desperate guerrillas
wave after wave of white mice
storm the beach and disappear
among the stones and pebbles

The weaker ones
retreat in confusion
hissing their bad luck, the steepness

At a distance
a reminder of yesterday's oil slick
glowers at me like a swastika;
nudged by a used condom
it elongates into the grim shadow
of a puritan
and backs away

A swimming girl laughingly
tosses
the floating rubber
on the back of a white mouse
scampering towards the shore

She straightens herself
in the water
and pulls up the wave
at her feet
like a turquoise slip

Coming towards me
she holds her breasts
as if they were brown puppies

PEACEMONGER

After our love-making
my Greek girl wipes the sweat
from my loins;
then she brings out chilled cucumbers and wine
and setting these before me
commands me to drink and eat.

Why doesn't everyone live
loving and carefree as we do
she wants to know,
a wrinkle appearing
on her forehead
tight as an unripe fig.

When I tell her
not all men are as lucky as I,
she says to lure them
from the battlefields
she would give her small, satisfying body
to all the armies of the world
— even those of Nasser and Hussein
or the despised Algerians

When I explain laughingly
that the chief attraction
is the chilled cucumbers and wine,
the wrinkle deepens to a frown.
'Ah, that presents a problem,' she says;
and my merry Greek wraps me around her,
spilling the white wine.

THE TRANSFIGURATION

She's gross and smells unwashed
and has the face of a natural breeder,
one full of good-natured smiles,
her blue eyes clear as those of a mindless nun
from one of the villages of Quebec;
there's a ridiculousness about her gait
as though she were a self-moving piano
pushing ahead, now one castored end now the other.
Why then when I saw her clumsying
down the narrow pathway that leads to the sea
in the warm gloom of twilight and could make out
only the grey outline of her stolid shape
why did I have a sudden vision
of her entering a mysterious transfiguring grotto
where, if I followed, a laughing slender goddess
would embrace me and it would be she?

MEMO TO A SUICIDE

When I was mad
about her
I bought all her daubs
— money on the barrel:
she wouldn't have it
any other way —
took her to expensive restaurants
movies and plays
lit up her body
with flowers and jewels
and with the fever
for an aging lover
threw in a summer's idyll
on the Riviera

You, Luke, hanged yourself
so that she could see
your blue tongue
sticking out at her
when she found you

TWO SONGS FOR SWEET VOICES

1

It was a late November day
Or so I dreamed a dream;
The fog descending on the banks,
The sun a frozen gleam.

No living thing survived except
That like a frightened thief
There quivered on a barren bough
A single, wind-torn leaf.

And only you and I, my love,
Remained to see it fall;
And you were very beautiful
And I was straight and tall.

And as sunlight ebbed away
We danced around the tree,
Until the snows came burying
The leaf and you and me.

2

Now all the fields are lying bare
And desolate;
The road, the gate
Address a sadness everywhere.

And you have pretty eyes to see
When Autumn comes
The lovely plums
Are taken from the crowded tree.

Yet should a kiss end my pursuit
I'd see again
The ripening grain
And all the trees bowed down with fruit.

LOVE POEM WITH AN ODD TWIST

Knowing
        that for as long
as I love you
  I shall stay
             merely a poet,
a babbler & word-spinner
  content to describe
or deride
        the bloody acts
of brave men
(Homer was my ancester)
        my self-revulsion
twisted into dagger
    or religious text
(which? let vanity
        or opportunity determine)
I've bought
      pistol
& black holster
    from an ex-Nazi
            For target
I've nailed
      a blown-up photo
of Nasser
     to an appletree
& each time I fire
    I shout, "I don't love
you": meaning
       you

AN AUBADE

It is early morning.
The cocks have stopped crowing.
The villagers are waking from dreams
of religious exaltation and buggery.
In their heads while shaving
or stirring their coffee
they carefully lock up their schemes
for profit and cuckoldry.
At the approach of this band of light
men arise to cheat or murder.
O wondrous Light! O wondrous Sun!
It has brought back their colours
to cowsheds and gardenias
to chickens and village dogs
who begin to squawk and bark
at their strange appearance.
From faraway mournful fields
the asses are braying,
'We want wimmin. We want wimmin.'
On the road the pellets of goatshit
look like stunted olives.
In other lands it is dark, dark.
North Ireland, Vietnam.
There light explodes like a bomb
or comes upon the night
like an assassin.
I sit on my bed and light a cigarette.
My girl is still sleeping.
When she awakes how will I
who read Husserl and Camus
tell her of my simple need of her
and that she must never leave me?

INSPIRATION

I have brought you to this Greek village
famed for its honey
as others are for their bread or wine
Love-making kept us awake
half the night
afterwards the jiggers took over
and would not let us sleep
Cocks and crowing women
woke us from our troubled doze
We compared laughingly the red bruises
on our arms and cheeks
Your good mouth, as it always does,
made me drool
and my spirit rose at once
In this stupid century
addlepated professors and mechanics
decry Inspiration
Alas, their arms have never held her;
gazing at you, woman,
in this shy early morning light I could more easily
doubt the feel of the bare boards under my feet
Truly this goddess has being
— in you , in some rare almost forgotten poems
and the mountainous hills and sea
which are waiting for us to look at them,
this vinestem curling on our windowsill
this bee
Come, let us show them
the fierce lumps on our divine foreheads

END OF THE AFFAIR

Wisdom is the decay of youth
but youth has no need of wisdom
being wise in its own fashion;
from day to day it lives the life
of instinct, sovereign passion
while the feeble with sober sense
tally both cost and consequence.
If another lay beside you
you would stroke his shoulders and arms
and he yours and the two of you
would be off to the hotel room
to make love. For that is impulse,
nature's wisdom, the rough wisdom
of the young who know enough
to tell their elders to be off
to their rocking chairs and blankets
or tranquilizing games of chess,
Monopoly or Plotinus
while they with hungry mouths embrace
whatever the moment and place.
But you and I like two scarred lovers
lie scared and inert on this beach,
an insult to the bright Greek sun
and the reproving water that
repeats its sad customary tale
for you grown old and wise and deaf
and me who look at you and sigh.

FAREWELL

She's gone. The one I swore up and down
to give a Greek villa and six children
if she married me, a trip around the world
to the moon. Mars, Venus
anywhere so that I could be with her
go great was the fire in my head,
in the sleeved arms that ached to hold her.

She's gone. The one that made me turn
restlessly from side to side each
sleepless night, thinking of her cool naked limbs
curled up on the lovestained sheets,
her red lips and long black lashes,
her smiles, her pouts, her sexy gestures,
the perfection of her small feet.

She's gone, whose laughter made me forget
the decorum of grey hairs,
children, friends, literary foes
the importance of being Trudeau, Pompidou, Spiro Agnew
or even the illustrious dust of Uncle Ho.
Let the whole world be damned, I said
and let the dead marry off the dead.

She's gone in whose arms I rose
resurrected after the third lay;
peace and wild joy and laughter were mine
for awhile but she's gone, gone in a bus
that with a snort has taken her far away
while the grey dust that settles over me
swirls and twirls like the ghost of an empty day.

FOR ANNA

You wanted the perfect setting
for your old world beauty, postwar Hungarian:
a downtown Toronto bar sleazy
with young whores pimps smalltime racketeers

remembering boyhood Xmases in Elmira
plus one poet pissed to the gills
by turns raving or roaring like an acidhead
then suddenly silent like the inside of a glass

I'm sure you placed him there as camera
as incorruptible juror or witness
but who can give report of a miracle?
having seen it what struck dumb can he tell?

and to whom? they who pressed around you
were converted and left off dreaming of murder
or rape in public parks/some cried for happiness...
they outside or riding the subways will never believe

Now I know everything which happened
that night was your creation/you invented
it all by cupping your elegant proper hands
then letting the night escape like a black moth

that shattered the fantastic radiance of your head
into a thousand glints and scintillations
transfiguring bottles whisky glasses even the leers
on aroused Canadian clerks fingering their wallets

and making me run after you to discover
whether you are a woman with blood and orifices
one may after all love and if the answer is yes
whether you will warn my aging limbs as a lover

PROTEUS AND NYMPH

I put down my book
    and stare at the distant haze;
the loud-voiced Greeks around me
    chomping on their fish and *peponi*
must reckon I'm having age-old thoughts
    on the human condition.
Noisy fools. I'm thinking of the waves
    gently cupping the breasts
of the lovely nymph just risen form the sea
    and the water lapping
her thighs and her delicate love-cleft

When she swims away
    she pulls my thoughts after her
in watery streaks of light. I become
    the sea around her
and she nestles in my long green arms
    or is held in the flowing
wavelets of my white hair. I billow
    above her like a dolphin
stroke her limbs and nip her rosy neck and shoulders
    with sharp unceasing kisses
till languorously she slips to the ribbed sand
    where under the haloing starfish
fern weed and enamoured seasnake I quiver
    between her silver thighs

SEDUCTION OF AND BY A CIVILIZED FRENCHWOMAN

Having agreed that Simone de Beauvoir's feminism
is a bad joke
that Sartre is a has-been and a stupid
Jansenist muddlehead
that Camus possessed more integrity than talent
that there are no longer any poets in France
worth mentioning
that much the same could be said for her novelists
and that, in general, French culture
is in a parlous condition, if not actually dead
not having cared to move
a single centimetre beyond Flaubert and Valery
and that no one except the two of us
seemed to know what is happening to that wretched country
having agreed politely to disagree
about Hemingway, Rimbaud, Holderlin, Nietzsche,
     Brecht, Lawrence,
Moravia, Jaspers, Kafka, Strindberg, and Pasternak's
     Dr. Zhivago
having dismissed politics as a *bêtise* and religion as a *folie*

AND

Having inevitably but cautiously left the high ground
of literacy and philosophical discussion
to speak of more personal, more mundane matters
i.e., one's dissatisfactions with conventional marriage, one's
adulteries, fornications, venereal diseases (there were none)
and given a desription of the circumstances attendant on one's
best and worst fucks

having slyly dropped two or three hints
about one's favourite erogenous zones and the best means
for stimulating them
and having led form this to the over-riding, paramount
        need in sex for
tenderness, mutual esteem, humour, *délicatesse*
        and for similar though
not necessarily identical tastes in literature, music, philosophy,
art, theatre, and contemporary films
we are now ready to make love

TO MARGARET

Aeons ago the African sun blackened your skin;
Africa looks through your eyes, walks on your elegant feet,
And Africa is in the suppleness of your limbs:
But the lope your serve me with— where is that from?

Let's see, your father was a Lowlander, your mother
Half Portuguese, half Kaffir black; and yet other
Strains are in you, did you say: French, German?
Truly an ingathering of nations under your own sweet skin!

Yes, sunk somewhere beneath your restless waves
Are the Dutch galleons, the Portuguese men-of-war;
And from time to time I can hear the tides pluck at them,
Turning them over stilly in their deep forgotten graves.

Luckily it's Africa predominates, shows through:
In your sureness, melancholy, ease and laughter.
You are a medley of many bloods, my dear mixed-up Margaret
But the puma that pads into my bedroom is wholly you.

DISCOTHEQUE

Hey, I want a ringside seat
on that ass
with no one crowding me

It's an action poem
                        a wrecker's ball
made wholly of air

That ass is pure magic
an invisible hypnotist
is swinging
                        from side to side
to hook me
                        on posterior analytics

I feel I'm going wall-eyed
into a trance

All I want to see
is that split-off dactyl
in cheeky faded-blue jeans
leaping out at me

It's a hopped-up pendulum
flicking out
                        the frenzied seconds
for all of us

To that relentless thump
all the quaint escritoires

                        of the past
are being carted off
& dumped into the waves below:
religion government philosophy art

On the floor of the discotheque
it's the tough heart-muscle
of the universe
                  I see
pounding eternally away

FOR FRANCESCA

Francesca
you have the name
of a woman
who should be my lover

I cannot sleep
and retell your name
over and over

The three syllables
make a music in my ear
no one has heard before

They ignite each other
into a flame
that lights my room's darkness
till I think the night has gone

The dawn comes
when I open wide my window
to let music and flame
astonish the whole world

CHANGELING

In my arms
you become again
a Russian

Germany
your neat one-and-a-half room apt.
in West Berlin
your work for the newspapers
drop in quiet folds around the bed

Your pubis
is a warm granary
in the white bareness of your body

I watch the gradual return
of your homeland
in the midnight blooming of your breasts,
in the transformation
of your mouth and chin: the primness
all gone

Your laugh
is a sunlit Ukrainian wheatfield;
your kisses are music
coming unexpectedly form behind
closed windows

More than half your life
lies in ruin

As summoning the lust
of a young Tolstoy
and sentences
from our favourite Russian
authors
I drive into you again and again

FOR MY INCOMPARABLE GYPSY

The beauty that nature would fill
with pregnancies I'd keep sterile
forever, to be gazed at, not touched:
a poem, a canvas under glass.
What has the fine curve of your chin
the trim perfection of your thighs
to do with ripening and decay?
Your tongue-kiss drives all sense away;
touch: my member salutes the world.
By such old contraptions nature
infests our disgruntled planet
with newsprint-reading imbeciles
with costive runts scribbling verses
and ugly girls who make me ill.
The world is turning brassier
and brassier. Plain decency
has disappeared into limbo
or wherever it is virtues
no longer fashionable go;
madmen would abolish classes
and the law of gravitation
with one reckless stroke of the pen,
and the inflamed ignatzes cry
for muscleman or psychopath
to hive them in honeyed cages
where theirs is but to eat and die
and no throwback appear
to make them feel inferior.

From here on in it's all downhill,
downhill all the way. Fine manners,
love and poetry and what once
went by the name of form or style
— all have been rammed up a baboon's
red asshole. Or Hitler's. The world grows
each day safer for knaves and goons.

So my incomparable gypsy
I decline the invitation
your amazing body sends me,
though brain and instinct are programmed
to infecundate all beauty.
Go fuck and fill your womb with child,
in these lines you'll never grow old
but stay as fresh as the first kiss
you pressed on my impatient lips.
Marriages are for common clay;
for you I wish eternal day
not pukes and the rounded belly.
Only in this embalming poem
my unravished beauty be mine.

THE PUMA

You are mistaken, he said
I am neither lecher nor womanizer.
If I'm crazy about women
it's for the beauty
some pitying devil threw over them,
a beauty that blinds my gaze to everything
except lips eyes breasts
and roils my blood
like a delicious venom.

When the fit is on me
I am their slave, their man Friday;
they can do with me as they will
and to their absurdest wish
I am as malleable as putty,
more pliant than straw.
For their ally is not beauty alone
But the scantness of sense or purpose
I find in the remotest curved niche
of the universe;
whoever framed its empty immensities
didn't reckon on a man's reason or conscience
or the unassuageable ache in my heart.

Women and poems are my sole chance here
to give expelled breath shape and contour
and fable it with meaning.
I place on the brow of every woman I love
a crown made from the choicest words;
I dress her like a woodland queen
in trope and metaphor.
My desperation blossoms into garlands
braceleting her wrists, my sick despair
into flowering anklets.

I plug the void with my phallus
and making love on bed or carpet
we transfigure pitchblack nothingness
into a tamed puma whose whiskers
we stroke between enrapturing kisses.

POET AND WOMAN

I can make poems only out of chaos,
out of hurt and pain.
I sing loudest when my throat is cut.

And saying this,
I handed her the razorblade
she lovingly slashed my throat with.

After, when she was sluicing the blood
into the enamelled urn
my sorrow was that I could not thank her.

Nevertheless out of that silence
my greatest poem was born: the one
she sings to the hairy Cyclops on her bed.

FOR MY DISTANT WOMAN

I remember you as your were in Paxi,
my distant woman, and send my disconsolate thoughts
handspringing backwards like a clown eager for plaudits
to pick up your scents again, your smiles, your tenderness.

Agile and talented, he will never catch up with you
though to nudge him harder I've promised him top billing
in a floodlighted arena of his own choosing:
not even the cleverest dog could pick up your scent again.

My absent darling, fragrance and tenderness are strewn
on the silver ripples we both watched one night
when the full moon and all the stars were listening to us:
they cling to whispers beyond the reach of dog and clown.

Your blurring image enters my nostalgia softly
as the sun's semen enters the crimson flowercup
and often, as now, like the first heavy gout of rain
that makes it toss and shiver on its tender stem.

IN PRAISE OF OLDER MEN

It's a good thing Picasso's dead:
my darling loves only old men,
grey-haired and decrepit.
I can offer specs and a hearing-aid
but what are these matched against
an authentic octogenarian? I dread
any dotard who comes hobbling towards us
lest he totter into my beloved's arms
to suckle her breasts with his infant's gums.
Despite my sixty-odd years
my wrinkles are too few, my back's
not bent enough
my ways too rough and vigorous
to ravish my darling.
I must wait for the slow days
to pummel me into her fondness,
cunningly devising meantime
shifts and wiles
to keep her from clapping soulful eyes
on my most feared rival, Mr. Artur Rubinstein
whose silvered hair haunts me like a nightmare.

OF THE MAN WHO SITS IN THE GARDEN

You went away. For the last time
the hotel doors received and enfolded you
like a lover's arms. I was left standing
in the dark street like someone too dazed
by a car's sudden illumination to move,
imagining your ascension and the key
being turned to let you in, the blaze
you switched on revealing my empty place.
Did your lips tremble as mine did
when I turned down the silent street toward
the Byzantine church, our impeccable cue
to quicken step that we might ravenously
lock in an embrace and kiss hands, mouth, eyes
in the shadows a stone cherub had made for us?
When our lips touched did the cherub blow his trumpet?

On this island full of boats and trinkets,
of failed expatriates without love or joy
I remember another island and another day:
music, laughter, tenderness of eyes and hands,
the whitewashed square full of horny Greeks
made still hornier yet by your walking by,
your full uplifted breasts lifting their tools
till it seemed tables and backgammon boards
must topple unless their fine upstanding members did,
your quick stride luckily making the crisis pass
as swiftly as it arose with no boards smashed
or Greeks, young and ancient, cursing a ruined game.
More proud than the Sheba-escorting Solomon
or pint-sized Napoleon making it with Josephine,
I was Paris and you were my enchanted Helen.

In the purpling dusk I softly call your name
and quite bonkers think from behind that shuttered house,
or that stone, or the dark solitary cypress
that towers above the aerials standing perched
on the rooftops like an army of Martina birds
you must appear, so vast the longing in my arms,
the wild hungry hope in my staring eyes.
Soon the ballerina stars will come dancing out
as if on cue, and under the glittering diversion
they make the guerrilla shadows linking massive hands
will darkly commandeer, my tremulous darling,
all your hiding places: cypress, stone, and house,
and push you into the garden where I sit writing this
and where each night under the speechless gaze of the moon
I bury my grizzled head between your naked thighs

SMOKE

I've come to the tavern
to wipe away
with the back of my hand
your face your caresses
and your perfume

How many glasses
will it take
before you become
as insubstantial
as the smoke form my cigar,
a grey chaotic turbulence
billowing into oblivion?

You are as unshakable as death
you accompany me everywhere
like my own death
that is waiting for me
in a villa
or a Roman convent
where guarded by simple nuns
I shall write out
my theology of despair

When the memory of your hand
lingers on my shoulder or arm
when the recollection of your kiss
reddens my lips and cheeks
and the pupils of my eyes
distend with curve
of your eyelashes
I begin to tremble
as if a shadow
had fallen across my grave

I am the stillness
I am the chewed cigar
I am the emptied glass
I am the scattered ash on the floor
and I am the grey smoke
that wreathes your beloved image
forever and forever
though it drifts and dissolves
in the white morning sunlight
that comes from the doorway
to falter on table and bar

THE QUILL

I am a caster on love's quill
a rotor on love's pin or spool
I am a whirling jack
on a greased mandrel

The band that kept me turning
in uniform motion with you
has snapped and flaps noisily
on the ground

I am still turning
with the same velocity
but the motion without control
is wobbly and uncertain

Soon, very soon,
I shall stop turning
and be deadstill

GONE

Lover, where are you?
The distant sky swallowed you up
in the roaring toy box
and you disappeared into it gulps.

It was a blank sky I saw
a cold dawn-white sky, suddenly empty
and so vast and overspreading
I could write my grief on it.

Without you laughing beside me
the expresso was acid on my tongue
as its blackness rushed out like a noise
to envelop the frenzied airport.

Where are you, lover?
I look through the kitchen window, stare;
the tall backyard trees and hedges
are a green unanswering wall.

HIDDEN WORLDS

My young dog barks at the snowflakes:
white mice, they parachute down form the sky
in terrifying numbers, assault his fine head
and brown coat, drive him into the shed

Where he trembles out of cold and bewilderment.
His first November, his first snowfall.
My neighbour's house is sullen. Bitter.
The unbandaged shingles are streaks of stale blood

And each unlighted window stares back at me
with the suspiciousness of an old woman
though inside my head Artemis is dancing
and a god readies himself for his resurrection

A patch of snow. Greenery. On a ragged leaf
the season curls up and dies
as a surviving fly crawling on the windowpane
opens a road for us to oblivion

You are far away. On another continent.
A spider's filament connects our hidden worlds.
I think of you reading a poem, smiling
and suddenly the grass is white with white lilac petals

THE LAST DRYADS

Though I've never been there I know you're on those hills
And from casements I've never seen you wave your hand;
When the boat moves past some lone cove I see you stand
And send a smile to me on the water's white curls.

When I reach out to touch you, you become sunlit air
Or the salt freshness of a solitary spray
That washes over my ankles and slides away;
Or I feel you beside me though you do not stir.

The dazzling columns lie shattered, the temples ruined;
The smiling deities they once held, all are dead;
Grim superstition dissolved them and in their stead
Men kiss bleeding wounds and thorns; ill they are and blind.

But you are nimble in every island I see,
Being the sole fair dryad to avert the blight;
Your light feet on their wharves is all there is of light
Yet see how from His gouts now bloom enemones!

MADMAN ON MITHYMNA BEACH

My love, I can take everything
the world throws at me
    except your silence.
When I do not hear from you
the sun's only a distant fireball
and the sea nothing but an old gossip
repeating *ad nauseam*
    her one good story
to the impassive beachstones at my feet.

I try to fill up the silence
with recollections of your smile
    and perfect mouth,
your humourous melancholy eyes;
and sometimes I play with it
as if it were an accordion,
stretching and closing it between my hands
    to squeeze form it dear sounds
or I put it to my lips like a flute.

Ah, like a madman wanting
to strike fire from air I want
    to make your silence speak;
no, sing, whistle, hum, call me endearments
and whisper hoarse words of love
so that I shiver with remembered ecstasy.
My head resting on a stone for pillow
    almost I catch your voice, love,
until comes again the ponderous sea.

LADY ON THE PIAZZA

This morning I had spaghetti
àl pomodora with your wraith
after we'd greeted each other
at the Piazza di Spagna

It had your perfect mouth
your smiling melancholy eyes
and stroked my hand without cease:
smiles fell on me from the air

Who thought of thievish Romans
the violence in the streets
or in one's own soul?
Once more you worked your miracles

Only when I pressed against you
did you recede and disappear
and my aching fingers embraced
a vanishing waistline of air

Love, so long as I draw breath
this city is you, and I shall always see you
sitting on the steps of the Piazza
surrounded by flowers and ruins

FOR ARTEMIS

When my merry village Greek
naked and bronzed by the sun
    lies down beside me
all the sea's pulses throb
with my great excitement
and I imagine the shadows
the surrounding rocks throw
    on the deserted beach
silent goat-footed satyrs
about to drag her into caves
    no human foot may follow

She is so lovely and desirable
I am an immortal god
    and I know with certainty
death is unreal, mere shadow-face
of sexuality, a foolish illusion
like the days and years men have invented
out of pride or idleness
    My hands are all over her
and when she bends into my body
I sigh and can no longer hear
    the gentle suck-suck of the sea

SNOWDRIFT

How can my mind encompass
a world of wolves
                      flashing murderous smiles
and credit cards
and you whose lips are of such perfection
they are an amulet
                      against all evil?

Mind can but can the heart, the heart?

This freezing December day
                      you gone
I imagine I am in coldest Siberia
and the yelling slavering pack
is gaining steadily on me
as my flying sled rushes
towards the dark snow-covered woods.

My fugitive Love
only when I see their bared teeth
will I fling them an arresting image
of you and me
                      scooped from this city
so full of us whispering kissing laughing
every flume ravine and avenue
lies under a snowdrift of memories.

DAVID AND BATHSHEBA

She gave herself to me and I was her god,
her king: nothing I did or could do
was ever mistaken or wrong. I was her Messiah
among men, tall and well-favoured and strong

As for my near-faultless psalms
in praise of the Lord and men of valour:
over their exulting strains she went simply mad
and would listen to them hour after hour

As God hears me, when I was frightened or sad
I was wise enough in the ways of woman
to keep away from her, aware compassion in women
puts to rout all urgings of desire

Yet before the new moon was in the sky
she was mousing out my frailties, scanning my troubled soul
for lesions and cracks. I took my harp from the wall
and sang to sleep the froward slave and infidel

THE PERFECT MOUTH

Never, I swear,
    in all my travels
did I see lips more perfectly shaped
so yielding, so soft,
the curve of them driving me
    out of my mind;
as did her chin's roundness

Hear me everyone:
    whole nights I could not sleep
for thinking of her perfect mouth
and in broad daylight
I'd stare at the subtle full lips
    like a blind man
who has just been granted sight

If I can have a last wish fulfilled
    I'll ask to see once more
the carmined orifice
that held me enslaved for so long.
I would forgive all, all,
    lies and mouth honour and deceit
on lips so perfect and beautiful

And watch once more the rose petals
    open on my manhood to distil the familiar perfume,
making my frame twist with pleasure
as she draws the sperm into her faultless mouth,
    the final spasm
turning into my death quiver

ONE DAY IN THE LIFE OF PINCU LAZAROVICH

My dearest Harriet,
no matter how the universe unfolds this day,
commencing precisely at 8:36 A.M.
it's good to know
as you brighten the bedroom walls with your rising
whatever butcheries, train wrecks, civil wars
and other evils
the remorseless clock tick-tocks into being;
whatever mocking lines history shoves into the mouths
of its wound-up puppets
— the evening newspaper throwing the jackpot
into your lap when you jerk down the handle:
ostpolitik, detente, people's democracy —
lying secure among the day's villainies
and vile accidents
there will be your surpassing loveliness, a flower
opening beyond the swamp's reach
for my eyes to take in with reverence and delight,
the certainty of our mounting desire
and passionate embrace
before the sun slides into the ocean
crimsoning with the day's shed blood.

THE CONVERT

Just when my faith is strongest
and I embrace Emptiness
with the fervour of a pill-popping
fanatic of Bay Street;
just when I know
beyond any shadow of confusion
ailing or demented people
are praying to a Chimera
and lighting futile candles for him
in hoary churches and cathedrals,
just then he turns his head
to smile goodness and peace at me
with your full perfect lips
and at that instant
I fall down on my knees
an awestruck convert,
my eyes two candles glimmering
in the dark

CLICK, CLICK

She makes a form out of fallen leaves
and is piqued
the wind brings them alive
on the grass
before she clicks them into eternal stillness

She wants
she waits patiently
for the moving air to go elsewhere:
gently patting their raggedness into place,
finger poised for the exact and perfect moment

Her face is beautiful
like glowing sculpture
and beautiful her hair,
the colour of turning leaves
warm and russet all around her

The god in the white clouds
the god in the vermilioned trees
the god in the gathered shadows
the god who is everywhere
gazes at her with my eyes

A million wavelets
climb the lakeshore rocks
or scatter between them
to tell the naked trees and her
he's shaking with ecstasy

Click

St. Marguerite, Quebec
September 25, 1978

FOR HARRIET

I am a matchflare
you are another
      Together
for an instant
we pierce the surrounding
dark

Two matchspurts
I'd have us be
      Not wicks
that flicker
to extinction
and black silence

I love all passing things:
roses and dust
      Their brief stay,
like your smile, instructs me
to embrace the world
with irony and joy

ORTHODOXY

God is omniscient
for he knows
I can love only one who smells good
and has responsive nipples

Knows, too, the hue of cheek
I adore above all others
and how maddened I am by a pout
on a perfect mouth

He is omnipotent
for he plucked you from ancient times
when fairest beauties were
and placed you here

And he is all-merciful
for how barren would be my days
were you not mine
to delight and amaze

RETURN TO EDEN

You were sent to me
so that I could make my declaration of love
beside a royal palm
and afterwards kiss your small ears
under the chorisia's white floss.

But everything that happened to me
before this
— what was all that about?

FOR SANDRA

Frenzied in my rented room
as I live and scarcely breathe
    I can think of nothing
but your blue fabulous eyes
your rounded full breasts
    and the fragrance of your hair
each time you moved or turned your head;
the delicious parts you let me kiss
and those you covered with a dazzling smile

It is 4 A.M.
and sleep is far from my tired eyes
    I am an insomniac
with a pen in my hand
a lunatic praising your beauty
    over and over again
to the framed darkness outside
and the frantic insects
scrabbling on the window-screen

Did you, O lovely lady,
really unhook the interposing bra
    and taking my hand
to your alerted nipple
did you, holding it there, really whisper
    after a long surrendering kiss
'I did that for my own joy, Love, not yours'
— or have I fallen asleep at last
and am I dreaming this?

THE CHASTENING YEARS

A long time ago
I contemned the middle class,
loathing their crassness, their incurable philistinism

Then it was the prole,
seeing what a bent pin he is,
the ever-obliging tool for masters

Later I observed to friends
that though a few fevered souls
cared vehemently for freedom and uprightness
the many-too-many in all lands,
the superfluous ones,
think mainly about stuffing their craws

Now with the innocent guile
the chastening years bring
I have resolved to keep in mind
only your fabulous blue eyes and smile
and to live as though nothing else matters
but the delicate play of your hands

FATA MORGANA

Perhaps tomorrow but not today, not now,
I'll smile at the grotesque picture I have
of myself sitting on your broadloomed floor
and reading poems to you, setting off
a jubilee of flambeaus and girandoles,
of conceits and happy valley fantasies
with a lover's fond rant Byron's hero
might have envied in his Venetian prime.

For you're as mad as they come, my dear,
and had not itch or vanity bewitched me
and the astonishing beauty of your face
I'd have read accurately the telltale signs
on your mouth, the blankness of your blue eyes
when you suddenly fell silent and only
your uneasiness and paranoia
rushed in to fill their sad vacancies.

At that moment I was an idiot babbling
to an imbecile, a ludicrous old fool
entertaining with trope and metaphor
a sick Aphrodite sighing on her sofa
whose only signal that she still lived
was a muffled cry of pain and horror
like someone startled into strangled speech
by her own foul dreams and apprehensions

May my rabbinical ancestors forgive me
but I groan aloud and grow pale remembering
how I gently put your hand in mine, saying:
'I'll work hard to be worthy of your love.'
Lofty declaration to a moping screwball!
O the folly a poet will say or do
when a woman's beauty ravels his senses.
O the squalid comedy of his blinding love.

But you are the world each poet courts,
prodigally expending his ardour and wit
on her service, transfiguring her dullness
and forever reading immense subtleties
into her vacant depthless stares,
the slow lunatic smile on her lovely lips.
So pardon's the word, my sweet bedlamite,
and may all your dreaming be of peace and joy.

BONDED

With you gone
I embrace pain,
pleasure's indisseverable twin

I would not unpartner them
even if I could

And I can't
             with you gone
and I, in our bed,
alone

"Do not look back
upon the lady when you lead her up from Hell;
disobey, she'll vanish into air, become invisible.

"Never again will you behold her face or form."

I was that singer who heard the gods and obeyed.
I charmed my lady out of Old Forest Hill
where her mother's baubles glittered like devils' eyes.

Not even her father's condo in Palm Beach could keep
that lovely shade.

She was all mine, following me with a bold surmise
from slagheap to slagheap as I played my reed.
I heard her light tread directly behind my own.

Though her nearness bewitched me, I did not turn my head.

O but I longed to see her dear face
more beautiful, perhaps paler, than asphodel;
to fall on my knees and kiss the folds of her dress.

To take into my lungs once more her fragrant smell.

At last looms before me the grim portal white with dawn.
My foot touches the earth beloved of living me.
I turn eagerly to embrace my love. She is gone.

At the mouth of Hell, once more I stand bereft, alone.

Though I had held the gods above the woman I prized
    and burned for,

the promised guerdon, a woman's love, was not mine.
Here nothing is certain and chance or accident rule
everything.
Now, more fiercely than ever do I pluck my lyre and sing.

OF LEAVES AND LOVES

Once a seed, now a tree crowned with leaves
that soil and sun, a principium of individuation,
shaped to hang for a summer and then fall.

Stars moulder and rot at a slower rate
or blaze suddenly into blackness
only to bud again on God's unfolding arm.

So my love was a quick seed
whose soil was your smile, its sun your joy.
A sudden frost turned its leaves black.

Black as the black night at my window.
No star will return to pierce the darkness.
No leaf ever bud on my withering stalk.

BLIND MAN'S BLUFF

The long dark September nights are coming,
reminding the vacant poet of losses;
there are no stars in his skull,
only blackness, the fumes of dead loves.

Jerusalem is ruined and pillaged
and her kings and queens are grimacing marionettes.
Where is majesty? Beauty? The courtesies of love?
The stiffening valour in sinew and thigh?

They lie unnoticed on his kitchen floor:
broken pieces of wood, the colours dissolving
into echoes a rising wind amplifies
to a pitch his wearied heart no longer hears.

After each night's solitary meal
he plays blind man's bluff with shadows
that recite lines from his own poems
to mock him as he reaches out hands to touch.

Old poets know that game well.
Designs of soft vulvas cover the walls. Only when
he removes the tight blindfold from his eyes
will a fleshless mouth kiss him with his own passion.

WHEN HOURLY I PRAISED

When hourly I praised her perfect mouth
How could I have known, with lust besotted,
That Satan himself had forged those red lips
To singe my wings, to crisp me like a moth?

OUT OF PURE LUST

for Vivian

The tight sweater she was wearing
showed off her good points at once;
luckily she had an attractive mouth
that lifted my thoughts so that my mind
raced to it from her twin attractions,
settling on neither long enough
to put a glaze on my devouring eyes.

At twenty-one she was explaining for me
why nobody wrote love poems anymore.
"Love's unsatisfied lust, nothing more.
If I want a man I jump into bed with him.
Who needs his heated fantasies, or mine?
I've learned a thing or two about poets:
the only sheets they soil are those they write on.

"If a lover has been fondling my breasts
why should he wish to dream about them
or cudgel his brains to put my nipples into a poem
when he can pop them into his mouth
like ripe berries? I prefer it, mister, that way.
So does he I'm sure, my breasts are so round and firm."
She stopped and I've wondered what old Petrarch would say.

Oh lecherous Alighieri who made his Beatrice
immortal by putting his lust into an Inferno.
What if she and Petrarch's Laura had been a good lay
and spoke of their lovers as they might of artichokes,
of ecstasies and fiascos, one-night stands,
finding the comedy of sex too funny for words?
What masterpieces would each have ripped off then?

THE BREASTSTROKE

for Diane Parent

May the gods be praised that I should meet
on my final lap to the eternal sea
one so young, so gracious and lovely,
under clear skies promising as herself.
Ankled deep in the scorching sands
I can hear the shouting tide; in it
invitation and menace like the smile
on the fair face of my companion,
making me wish to nuzzle forever
between her firm thighs and cover
her mouth with long hungering kisses.

Insensate to everything but her warm flesh
I'd float out into the voluptuous sea,
my practised breast stroke perfect at last.
The heaving mounds press against me,
alluring me past the white wavecrests
that close behind like tall portals
barring return. Green towers collapse
on bright medallions larger than suns;
the virginal foam breaks into bridal cries
and after the last loud crash of savaging breasts,
into the long silence that no man hears.

Cuba
December 30, 1981

ODD OBSESSION
for Lisa

I've seen your singular smile elsewhere.
On sun-warmed Mediterranean statues
of the late Alexandrian period.

With your fragile, ever-smiling lips you appear
both sensual and ascetic, a coin's toss
sending you either way.

The curves of your mouth bracket your secret.
Which are you? Mary, mother of Jesus,
or that other Mary, the scarlet Magdalene.

Your secret is that you don't know.
So you smile often to conceal your confusion,
giving you that strange look that intrigues us all.

Your lips obsess me like a misremembered word.
I can't remove them from my head, or imagine
any greater triumph than to blot them out forever.

At fourteen I made an older girl
articulate "prunes" over and over again
because her mouth shaped beautifully pronouncing it.

Yours, I finally conclude, is the smile of a woman
who, figure and face making her irresistible,
mocks her lovers' immoderate passion.

But mostly mocks the world and herself.

SEVENTEEN LINES AND THREE KISSES

for Veneranda

7 A.M. He switches the light on in the kitchen.
Pale yellow. The colour of beaten egg
mixed with milk, sunspots on all the walls.
He picks up a book to read. His woman
still keeps the stars in her head. She dreams.
Of what? Of the perfect existential lover
who will give he no more trouble. Of a love
that walks confident as an animal.
she has suffered so much from love, from men
who are not the right kind of animal. When
she gives herself she demands nothing more
than glasses brimming with red wine, and laughter.
What can she ever do with spilled wine
and broken glasses; with laughter that makes
a place nobody can live in except necrophiles
and warlocks?
                    He tiptoes into her bedroom
and leaves three sincere kisses on her pillow.

Montreal
September 16,1981

NEW YEAR'S POEM FOR VENERANDA

When she climbs the steps of her basement apartment
she leaves the place in absolute darkness
except for the small mirror in my mind
that holds her surprised reflection.

I polish it till her confident smile
lights up my eyes and when I whisper
in the dark: "I love you with all my heart,"
the corners of the room begin to shine.

She will bring wine and two goblets
and we'll toast my familiar daimons,
my obsession with her mad-making limbs:
cry window-breaking huzzas for her vagrant soul.

I've flicked off the years, one by one:
"This one loved me, this one didn't."
Tonight I'll give her the denuded stalk
and it will turn a sunflower in her hand.

Roxboro
December 31, 1982

VENERANDA DANCING

She dances like a solitary bacchante

The tight miniskirt she flicks
before my eyes
is a leopard's ever-changing
spots

On the crowded dancefloor
she dances like someone possessed
and I am lost to all
except the motion
of her disordering limbs

When she dances like that
I can follow her down
all the way down
into the smoky bowels of hell

RENDEZVOUS AT THE COFFEE MILL

for Sarah

Will you be as beautiful
    as I imagine you?
As sensitive and tender?
    Unloyal or true?
Will you have a sense of wonder
or will you be a pious clod
    imploring an ignorant god?

Few women delight for long.
    Most disappoint.
A sly malcontent
    lies wound up in each.
As I hope to live
a thousand years for my sins
    their poor souls are costive.

When I was young
    I adored every girl
that stopped my breath.
    I lived only for their smiles.
But hopes run with the years
and love brings to this life
    dissension and strife.

At this hour, only a name,
    still unseen, unknown,
time is weaving you
    on his loom of possibility.
When you emerge at 9 p.m.
fully shaped from his frame
    how will you greet me?

Who will you be?

YEATS AT SIXTY-FIVE

Your warty lads are too shy to tell you
they burn to cover your body full length.

But I, a white-haired lecher and famous,
boldly apprise the world I do.

Dear maid, which will pleasure you most:
a young man's shyness or an old man's lust?

TRAGEDY

for Annette Pottier

At my invitation
she comes to see me.
She is young and gorgeous.

And I am seventy
plagued by memories
and arthritis.

Let Lear and Oedipus rant
on all the stages of the world.
They were but blind old men.

I TAKE ANNA EVERYWHERE

I take my Anna everywhere.
She is so beautiful she can break
a man's heart with a look,
the proud thrust of her shoulder.

She tells me she will die young.
I tell her all beautiful women have the same
premonition. Brevity is the stamp
of beauty, sealing it in the mouths of men.

I take my Anna everywhere.
She has the unpitying gaze of a goddess.
All the men who see her
want to live their wrecked lives forever.

LADY AURORA

My woman is still sleeping.
Her face, the face of a goddess,
is pressed against the white pillow.

How long can I stand here
wonderstruck at her beauty
and filling my soul with her peace?

So long as I can hear her breathing
death will never touch my marrow.
Joy gives me the courage to live forever.

In her presence a troubled worm
is changed into a tall man
into a warrior who laughs at perils.

Soon the dawn will touch leaf and grass,
starting fires everywhere.
                    When she opens her eyes
I shall blaze more brightly than fern or bush.

A MADRIGAL FOR ANNA

The lioness leaps upon her prey.
The tyrant's teeth are white and strong.
The Apocalypse is on its way.
Saintliness keeps no one safe from wrong.
I, knowing the unloved man's a clod,
Let a woman's kisses warm my blood.

Man's foul breath corrupts the atmosphere.
The crimson'd earth inherits the meek.
The sick and dying are at our door.
All mortals rage to kill the weak.
I, knowing the loveless man's a sod,
Let a woman's mouth delight my blood.